MERCURY FLATS
PUBLISHING
AN IMPRINT OF
ATOMIC MOUNTAIN PRESS, LLC

BOOKS BY BEN DOUGLASS
PUBLISHED BY
MERCURY FLATS PUBLISHING

Beneath The Surface (Paperback)

The Last Cuppa: A One-Act Play
(Paperback)

Against The Grain: Poems of
Liberation (Paperback)

A Short Story Collection (Paperback)

THE RESTLESS SPIRIT:
A Spiritual Memoir

by Ben Douglass

THIRD EDITION
Mercury Flats Publishing, ABN
Copyright © 2026 by Ronald Dwayne Douglass
ALL RIGHTS RESERVED

Second Edition:
Douglass, Ronald D. (2016)
Confession of a Former Zombie.
Amazon Create Space

First Edition:
Douglass, Ronald D. (2014)
Confession of a Former Zombie.
Amazon Create Space

Library of Congress Control Number: 2026908525
ISBN: 979-8-234-04620-8 (Paperback)

Mercury Flats Publishing, ABN
[*an imprint of Atomic Mountain Press, LLC*]
5325 Northeast 37th Avenue
Portland, Oregon. 97211
Email: mercuryflatsgazette@gmail.com

Standard Address Number: 992-3705

Cover Design: MS Co-Pilot 365 (edited)
Logo Design: MS Co-Pilot 365 (edited)
Graphics: MS Co-Pilot 365 (edited)
Text Editor: Rene Walsh, Walnut Creek, CA.

Font: 14-point Verdana for Easy Reading

DISCLAIMER: The real names used in this memoir are those who are no longer living, but used respectfully. All other names have been changed to protect the living.

NOTE: The copyright holder of this work publishes under the pseudonym of **Ben Douglass**.

DEDICATION:

Barry Norman Mallet
1948 – 2012

A regular guy who survived the Tet
Offensive in Viet Nam, only to suffer
a lifetime of debilitating health from
his exposure to Agent Orange. He
was a true friend in every sense of
the word and will always be
remembered for his no-nonsense
attitude and his dreams that were
larger than life.

"Do I contradict myself? Very well
then I contradict myself, (I am
large, I contain multitudes.)"

Song of Myself
Walt Whitman

"If a man does not keep pace with
his companions, perhaps it is
because he hears a different
drummer."

Walden
Henry David Thoreau

TABLE OF CONTENTS

Forward by Rene Walsh, P11
Author Preface, P 15

1. Growing Up Absurd, P19
2. The Magical Mystery Tour, P43
3. Sex is Evil, Sex is Death, P69
4. From India With Love, P77
5. Buddha Ain't Here Anymore, P101
6. Becoming Human Again, P111
7. The Road Ahead, P121

About the Author, P125
Contact Info, P131
About Mercury Flats
Publishing, P133

FORWARD

There seems to be a particular loneliness that comes with outgrowing the faith that raised you: you don't just lose answers – you risk losing your people, your language, your place in the room. This memoir begins there, in that fracture, and refuses to look away. From an evangelical Christian upbringing certainty to Eckankar, then onward through two Hindu-based movements, into the quiet rigor of Soto Zen, to Humanism, and ultimately to a form of Radical Agnosticism, Ben Douglass' journey reads less like indecision and more like an unwillingness to lie – especially to himself.

I've known the author of *The Restless Spirit* for nearly half a century – we've been friends since 1977 – and I'm grateful for the chance to introduce these pages.

What follows is not a manifesto and not a clean and tidy conversion story. It is a record of a life honestly lived in the presence of big questions – about God, truth, belonging, authority, questions like "Who am I," "Where am I going," "How do I get there," and what it means to be awake in this world. He does not offer these *God-shopping shifts* in his journey as trophies. He writes about them as lived experience – complete with zeal, disappointment, relief, confusion, and the kind of doubt that isn't laziness but conscience.

What moved me most is the care with which he tells the truth about each stage without caricature. He can describe the comfort of certainty and the cost of it. He can honor sincere teachers while acknowledging how spiritual communities – any communities – can fail their own ideals. And he can admit when he was wrong, when he was naive, and when he was simply human. This is writing that refuses to score points; it tries instead to see clearly.

At its heart, this memoir is about integrity – the decision to keep searching when easy answers no longer ring true, and to keep practicing compassion even when one's metaphysical map is in question. Along the way you'll encounter the allure of belonging, the ache of losing it, and the surprising ways wisdom can appear in unexpected places: in prayer, in mantra, in sitting still, in service, and in the simple act of telling the truth to oneself.

Some readers may arrive with strong loyalties to one tradition or another. Others may come wounded, skeptical, or simply curious. Wherever you begin, I invite you to read with the same generous attention the author extends to his past lived times. His "radical agnosticism" is not a pose of superiority or a retreat into nihilism; it is, as he presents it, a disciplined refusal to pretend to know what he cannot know – and a commitment to live responsibly anyway.

This book won't tell you what to believe. It may, however, help you recognize your own longing for the real, your own grief over what falls away, and your own courage in beginning again. I'm honored to commend this memoir to you, and I hope you will meet it as I did: with an open mind, a steady heart, and a willingness to be changed by another person's honest account of seeking.

Rene Walsh
Walnut Creek, California
January 20, 2026

AUTHOR'S PREFACE

This memoir first began not as a grand vision, but as a frustrated scribble on several napkins at a Portland, Oregon coffee shop in 2006. I then published my thoughts on the matter in a twelve page essay ("God-Shopping") on a now defunct website in 2010. In 2014 I expanded that essay to 36 pages and published it on Amazon's Create Space Platform with the title, *Confession of a Former Zombie*. A second "revised" edition came out in 2016. And there it sat for 10 years.

This Third Edition you are holding has gone through many changes, including trim size, title change, bulking up each of the sections with new information and background to feed the reader a more premium reading experience. As before, names were altered unless that person was a public figure.

I wrote this book because I spent many years looking for something I could honestly call *true*. I didn't start out trying to become a skeptic. I started out trying to make sense of my life, my pain, my hope, and the question of whether anything – or anyone – was listening.

My story is not a conversion story. It's simply a road map of where I have been. My path started with Evangelical Christianity, New Age spirituality, two India-based movements, Soto Zen practice, and a season of committed humanism, before arriving – at least for now – at what I refer to as "radical agnosticism. I'm not presenting this sequence as a blueprint or a warning. It's simply what happened when I kept following my questions.

In these chapters I describe the practices, communities, and ideas that shaped me, along with the costs: the moments of clarity, the periods of disillusionment, the comfort I found in certain teachings, and the harm I experienced – or caused – when certainty outran wisdom. I've tried to be fair to each tradition I encountered, even when I ultimately couldn't stay there.

Thank you for trusting me with your time. I'm grateful to the people who listened, challenged me, and stayed in conversation with me – especially when my beliefs changed. If anything in these pages helps you feel less isolated in your own searching, or gives you language for doubts you've been carrying quietly, then this has served its purpose.

With Grace,
Ben Douglass
Portland, Oregon
April 5, 2026

PART 1
GROWING UP ABSURD

Like all humans, I am a complex biological system of skin, bones, chemicals, and mostly water. But I have never held that against myself. My entire life has been a testament of knocking on the door of *Absurdity* and screaming: "Hello!" Absurdity is the human tendency to seek inherent value and meaning in life and the human inability to find any.

The universe and the human mind do not each separately cause this absurdity, but rather, absurdity arises by the contradictory nature of the two existing simultaneously in space-time. The efforts of a nobody like me (and all the other little nobodies populating this place) to find inherent, universal meaning will ultimately fail because the sheer amount of information as well as the vast realm of the unknown make certainty impossible. And yet, however, I say one should embrace the absurd condition while conversely continuing to explore and search for a personal meaning that eventually makes life desirable and filled with joy.

This is not a story that dwells on people, places, and vital statistics. That kind of story is written by Presidents, famous Hollywood actors, astronauts, Nobel Laureates, serial killers, and TV preachers. When I was young, I use to tell people that I was simply a footnote in history. This was a very brazen attitude coming from a young boy who was a nobody, because even footnotes are more well-known than someone like me.

This story, my story is a narrative account about all the little deep and secret spaces while searching for meaning. That search in the face of the absurd could have driven me to alcoholism or suicide. Instead I chose another path that took me down many streets and dead ends in the realm of religiosity.

$$***$$

A small and mostly inaudible cry occurred at 3:53 pm on Friday, January 7, 1955 in the scrubby oak-laden foothills of Northern Napa county, inside a small and austere building that was half general hospital and half tuberculosis sanitarium. This was the absolute raw beginnings of life as I came to know it.

Sanitarium (Formerly Crystal Springs Spa) was an unincorporated community in Napa county, California. It lies at an elevation of 587 feet and located 2.5 miles north of St. Helena. The settlement was founded in 1878 by Seventh-Day-Adventists who opened a sanitarium called Crystal Springs. The community that grew up around it was called Sanitarium. The Sanitarium post office operated from 1901 to 1970, when it was removed and the town renamed Deer Park.

✳✳✳

I was born into a working-class, Protestant family who was always on the verge of economic disaster. My mother's people hailed from County Meath in Ireland. They were Catholic and tended towards liberal or cosmopolitan values. Most of them were imbibers of strong drink and generally sought to have a good time in life. When my mother married my father she converted to his Protestant faith.

My father's people hailed from Aberdeen, Scotland. They were staunch members of the United Brethren Church, which was a distance offshoot of the Mennonite Church. My father's parents were very strict teetotalers and also condemned smoking, dancing, games, and movies as sinful and a waste of time. When my parent's started their family they chose the Presbyterian Church initially.

The First Presbyterian Church of Napa was a Victorian Gothic-style building with a fellowship hall that was stunning to look at by a four-year old boy. I thought it was a fairy castle of sorts sent by God. The pastor was one Erwin Bollinger, who was known by most as "Bolly."

My great uncle Don Douglass and great aunt May were members of this church, as well as their children and grand kids. It seemed half the congregation was made up of my relatives. I loved that building as a small child. I would sit up in the balcony during Sunday morning sermons with other kids my age. One Sunday we got a bit noisy and that was the last time we were allowed to sit up there without parental supervision.

Pastor Bollinger was an amazing man which everyone respected. He seemed like a god dressed in his black robe and purple sash.

He was dynamic in speech and dress and that made a great impression on my young mind, especially when he would pat me on the head and give me that beautiful, radiant smile. I always felt safe and loved in his presence.

The best thing I remember about that church was all the nook and crannies to explore, and the giant pipe organ made the whole building shake. And there were many potlucks in Westminster Hall.

Around 1961 the family moved to Hayward, California, an hours drive from Napa. During my first and second grade years we attended the Westminster Presbyterian church, however, I have no memory of this at all. My sister, being seven years older had a complete memory of those first years in Hayward.

During the summer of 1964, we went on a family vacation across country to Pennsylvania and Ohio to visit my father's side of the family. After we got back my sister started visiting this church with a great youth group, so we switched churches. We started attending as a family that fall. It was called the Village Church of Hayward – an affiliate with the Christian and Missionary Alliance. The building on Mission Boulevard was quite funky and plain looking, nothing even near the grandeur of Napa's First Presbyterian.

The Christian and Missionary Alliance (C & MA) is an evangelical, Christ-centered denomination and global missions movement founded in 1887 by Pastor A.B. Simpson. It focuses on fulfilling the Great Commission by planting churches and sending international workers to bring the gospel to marginalized and unreachable people worldwide.

Because of my maternal grandmother's alcoholism and the fact that my mother took a barbiturate to control her epilepsy, she never drank. Whereas my father smoked cigars and joined the boys after work at the local bar and came home drunk several times a month. Years later I concluded that it was a release mechanism from his strict upbringing. Then one day at the age of nine the minister from the Village Church came to our house and had a long talk with my father, while us kids had to "go play outside."

After this visit my father quit drinking and smoking quite abruptly. We were really never told why – even in my later years it was shrugged off. I believe it had to do with a *vision* my father had and committed himself to Christ and family. I do remember my fathers behaviors and attitudes never did change much. He ended up being what is called a "dry drunk."

Even though neither of my parents finished high school, I was always given the opportunity to read and further my education. Twice I remember my parents purchasing encyclopedia sets for us kids to use for our homework or just reading pleasure. Though I was given the opportunity to advance my knowledge while growing up, the substance of that knowledge mostly conformed in every way to reinforcing the Christian worldview. I did, however break from that worldview, to discover new knowledge, which sent me on a life time of study.

During the summer of 1971, I was searching for answers to life and what my real purpose was on this spinning blue dot. I sought answers that the church was not or unable to give me. I became very dissatisfied with my Christian faith after reading Kersey Graves 19th century book, *The Sixteen Crucified Saviors*.

I realized that I had been living in a religious bubble and there were many more things to look at out there in the real world.

That summer, and the summers that followed, I would spend my time in the local library researching religion, philosophy, theology, ancient history, and occultism. I also became a regular customer at Bookland Bookstore – a used bookshop where you could buy books and then re-sell them back for credit (or cash) on the next purchase.

This hole-in-the-wall bookshop was owned by a secular Jewish couple, Ed & Margaret Lustig. I came to know them well and a few times went out for Chinese food with them and their two boys.

While perusing the religion section in one of the back rooms, I found a 1934 copy of George Sales translation of the Quran called, *Alcoran of Mohammed*. It was a hardcover edition in poor condition: yellowed pages and two big cracks down the spine. A huge, thick rubber band held it together. The price was $20 but the owner ended up giving it to me for only $5.

This was my first experience owning and reading the Quran. I spent that summer pouring over its pages like an investigative journalist, attempting to glean whatever truth could be found. This was also the summer I read *Autobiography of Malcolm X*. His story about social activism and becoming a Muslim fired up my imagination to continue my search exploring various religious paths.

Another delectable discovery at this time was *Autobiography of a Yogi* By Paramahansa Yogananda. This book had the effect on me like a match dropped into a bucket of gasoline.

The strange and wonderful tales completely overshadowed the science fiction stories that were a big part of my reading diet up to this point. The book, in a sense, was every bit like a fast-acting, highly addictive drug on a young mind that had insufficient training in skepticism and rational, problem-solving skills.

And yet another discovery at this time was *Fate* magazine – the premier metaphysical monthly of the day. I awaited each monthly issue with breathless anticipation. My parents looked upon it as a harmless past time, and an obvious continuum of my one-sided science fiction diet. This magazine became a valuable resource to connect to the world of the "strange but true."

The minister of my church noticed my fascination with the occult world literature. He enthusiastically encouraged my reading and was

gracious enough to open up his his
personal office library to me for my
extracurricular education.

Being the janitor of the church, I
spent much time in Pastor Taylor's
office over and above the required
ten hours weekly. Since I had keys
to the building I was permitted to let
myself into the ministers office
whenever I wanted to peruse his
books. Looking back I am certain he
did this so that he would have some
control and direction over my
reading material.

Unbeknownst to him this situation
just poured more fuel on the
transcendental fire within: and
within a direction that would
ultimately take me beyond the
church. For this I am forever
grateful to pastor Richard C. Taylor,
Sr. This minister, who was also the
church founder of our small
congregation of 50 members plus
kids, had a great impact on me

as a role model. Not only was he a man of God but also a veritable encyclopedia of strange, odd and exotic stories. He was also an accomplished magician who did tricks behind the pulpit to illustrate his sermons.

Pastor Taylor was a very moral man who went on several food fasts each year, supposedly in order to get closer to God. His office library, as well as the one in his home, was an astounding monument of the finest pseudo-scientific and pseudo-historical writings known.

It was here I first discovered Professor Arnold Ehret's *Mucus-less Diet Healing System* and Immanual Velikoesky's *Worlds in Collision*. Besides the traditional fare of books by Paul Tillich, Martin Buber and the early church fathers, he had exotic writings that didn't seem to fit his role as a fundamentalist preacher. It was these exotic treats

I spent most of my time reading; books on Breathetarianism, UFO's, ancient astronauts, the lost continents of Atlantis and Mu, ESP, etc. One might conclude I received a first-class Ivy League education in weird science, weird philosophy and weird history. It was not surprising then that the next step in my intellectual evolution lead me into the New Age movement like a Saturn 5 rocket.

The summer of 1971 was a very intense time for me theologically, emotionally, and psychologically. And not only was it a time of great social upheaval – drugs, music, hippies, sex, demonstrations, and riots – but it was an unbearably hot summer. My mother had been diagnosed with breast cancer and having a rough time of it following her mastectomy. I nearly lost my mother that year and it had a huge emotional impact on my small provincial world.

As I stated before, Kersey Graves 19th Century book, *The Sixteen Crucified Saviors*, had a profound impact on my Christian faith. Everything I had taken for granted about Christianity was thrown back into my face as just one of many mythologies in the world. I still remember to this day the feeling of anxiety and dread with much poignancy.

The worst thing about this new dilemma was that I had to keep this a secret. My emotional bond with the church and family was too important to jeopardize at this point. I promised myself that I would continue my own search for truth while maintaining a good front until I graduated high school and left home. I did ask certain burning questions of a theological nature to those in authority but they either didn't know or refused to offer any explanation.

One of those burning questions that was never answered was about so-called out-of-body experiences. Since 1964 I had been having strange falling and flying dreams that were so lucid that they sometimes frightened me. When I put this information to pastor Taylor he would grimace and think a bit and finally say, "Maybe you should try out for softball or tennis and not think about those things all the time."

I really did not think about these things that much, regardless of Pastor Taylor's implied comment. Those experiences just happened and I needed to know why. Sometimes while sitting in a chair on a lazy, warm afternoon, I would slightly doze off and find myself flying about the room in some sort of light body. These experiences were always preceded by a sucking sound or cork being popped in my ear.

I always felt a sudden rushing sensation of my body as if I were being pulled out the top of my head. For a young fellow these were indeed strange and curious experiences. The worst thing of all is that nobody seemed to know what I was talking about, and if they did offer advice it was always an admonition to ignore it. This common response to my questions always shifted to why I "wasn't outside playing ball and getting some fresh air." This did not help me for I was having such vivid experiences and so desperately needed a reason behind this phenomenon. There was one person in my life that tried to be legitimately helpful by giving me his copy of Thomas Merton's book, *Contemplative Prayer*. He also lent me a copy of The Spiritual Canticle by *St. John of the Cross*. I, of course, read and studied these two volumes but still my questions weren't fully answered.

I sought my answers in the only direction I was familiar with: occult literature. Fate magazine was filled with stories of people having experiences just like mine. In the August 1971 issue of that magazine I saw a full-page ad about Eckankar – The Ancient Science of Soul Travel. The picture of Eckankar's founder, Paul Twitchell, sitting in yogic posture on a flying carpet above exotic temple domes totally captured my imagination unlike anything before. Even though my compulsion was to send off for membership, I did in fact wait awhile. At this point during my thirst for answers, I wish there had been someone who could have rightfully explained what was really going on with my flying dreams, for it could have saved me many years of wasted effort, time and money. If only someone had explained the basic principles of physiological-based psychology behind these experiences.

In late October of 1971, while prowling the shelves of science fiction at Bookland Bookstore, I came across a second edition of Paul Twichell's book, *The Tiger's Fang*. Looking back I still think it rather ironic that it was filed among the science & fantasy books. But then again, the owner, Ed Lustig, simply smiled at me when I paid and said, "That looks like a first-class fantasy."

This particular book was extremely pivotal in my decision to become a member of Eckankar. One month later I sent my hard-earned money to the Las Vegas based organization for two more books. The books arrived within three weeks. Enclosed with the books was a membership form and several pieces of promotional literature.

The information not only promised to explain my mysterious out-of-body experiences, but offered a course of instruction so that I too could become an Eck Master and roam the universe in my soul body unencumbered by this mundane and crazy, mixed-up world of 1971. It was the ultimate science fantasy story come true and I could be a participant.

What's really absurd about this time of my life, I was still faithfully attending Sunday church services and also Wednesday evening prayer meetings. And here I was studying privately something so profoundly and diametrically opposed to my born faith. I was also reading at this pivotal point in my life two books by Albert Camus, *The Stranger* and *The Rebel*. And yes, indeed, I was a complex youth. And much of this complexity has carried over into my old age.

PART 2
THE MAGICAL MYSTERY TOUR

On January 30, 1972, I received my official Eckankar membership card in the mail. It was a blur wallet-size card with five vibrating circles at the top. A gold star was already pasted in the first circle proclaiming I was a first initiate. I really felt special. My first monthly discourse was also enclosed. The price was certainly right at three dollars a month, which included a one-year discourse series, the Mystic World bulletin and of course "secret access to the higher spiritual worlds."

I spent the rest of that year buying every Eckankar book I could lay my hands on, and then absorbing the information like a dry sponge in water. I actually believed that in five years time I would have "startling spiritual powers" at my disposal to "fight the forces of evil and help usher in a new age of enlightenment for all humanity." I would be at the forefront of a vanguard of select human beings.

At this science fiction lost all its appeal. I suspected it was just a natural maturing of my reading habits but, Eckankar and its myriad publications became my ultimate fantasy come true. Eckankar offered a vast international network of information and people, and exposure to this started breaking down my provincial worldview.

New ideas, events and people rushed into my world like a swollen creek during a winter storm. I discovered new literary treats in the writings of Hesse, Ferlinghetti, Ginsburg, Burroughs, Strindberg, and much cutting edge pop psychology and sociology. I sold all my 300-plus science fiction book collection just so that I could invest in these other tempting treats. I also stopped reading all other spiritual literature quite abruptly because as the Eckankar party-line went: "we are above all that. We are on the direct path to God."

In fact, this classicist attitude in Eckankar was so strong that we all looked down our righteous noses at those people who were still mired in the lower worlds as "ordinary humanity."

Eckankar, founded by Paul Twitchell in 1965, was a new religious movement known as the Path of God-Consciousness, and Spiritual Freedom, which taught that individuals can experience the Light and Sound of God directly. Headquartered in Las Vegas, Nevada at the time, it focused on Self-Realization, karma, reincarnation, and "Soul travel" – the ability to travel in higher states of consciousness to achieve spiritual liberation in one's lifetime.

By February 1973, I decided to start acting on my new found faith in a subtle but substantial way. I was studying the teachings by myself via the mail and felt pretty isolated with all this energy so I sent away to the main office for a packet of brochures and posters. I felt this great need to proselytize this new truth anyway I could without bringing attention to myself.

I walked into my high school's office and got permission to hang a large poster on the hallway bulletin board. From the reaction I received from the secretary she didn't have a clue what the poster represented, and probably didn't care. The poster stayed up for several days and even survived the usual graffiti. When the Principle got back on campus from an out-of-town conference the poster was promptly taken down.

After this I kept putting up posters around the school on the sly.

After high school graduation I couldn't get out of the hose fast enough and move to Napa, California, where our family originally came from. My sister was already living there with her new husband and I had lots of relatives on my mother's side still there. My grandmother was in a rest home with a badly broken hip for the next six months, so my aunt Vera let me stay in my granny's flat rent free until I got my act together.

It was during this time that I consolidated and solidified my faith in Eckankar, and went on to accept several positions of responsibly locally. Those months presented many opportunities of personal growth as well as relationships with people I may never have met otherwise. What was astounding during this phase of my life was my unquestionable loyalty I gave to the organization and its leadership. I denied myself everything just so

I could reach the spiritually hungry masses with *truth*. I was on a mission. I was the secret agent of God. I was going to change history.

I quickly became an Area Representative for Napa County and was given the Fourth Initiation. However, I soon found that certain things about me as a person held me back and pushed me off the fast track to become an Area Mahdis (a Fifth Initiate that oversees an area and gives out initiations to others).

It seemed that those who advanced in the ranks weren't smarter or wiser than anybody else, or had stunning spiritual experiences, but it was based upon how often you sought the affection of the powers that be, which included agreeing with them on just about everything, from what type of soap you used to politics in general. I can still remember the really weird feeling I got when I out just how the recommendations for initiation actually happened, and the very arbitrary way individual Initiators did it.

I remember when given the Fourth Initiation by Laurie M., it was a sacred and moving moment and done in a professional manner. However, my Third Initiation in Walnut Creek at the Eckankar Center, Marilyn D., sat there with this silly little hat on her head for the ceremony. And when I opened my eyes briefly she was yawning and looking out the window. It looked bizarre and funny at the same time. My Second Initiation was also done with an air of solemnity and professionalism, but the initiator tried to sell me her favorite line of vitamins right after the ceremony.

Another bigger reason I stayed in the Fourth Circle of Initiation for seven years to the bitter end was my politics.

From 1974-1979, I was a dues paying, card carrying member of the Socialist Workers Party of America. I even sold the party newspaper on the streets of San Francisco at least a dozen times. Eckankar never told me directly that being a member of the S.W.P.A was forbidden. Eckankar seemed to go out of its way publicly to say, "the individual's politics was their own personal business." But what happened in reality was an entirely different matter.

Some Eckists (that's what we called ourselves) I came across were either very conservative politically or most just didn't give a shit about voting or issues. When my fellow Eckists found out about my political affiliation and activism they often took the approach that I was somehow wasting my time and had fallen into the "claws of Kal Niranjan" (Satan).

This love affair with Eckankar ended in 1983. What happened next was dramatic as well as traumatic for most members. The darkest and saddest day in the history of the movement began. Sri Darwin Gross was excommunicated by his chosen successor, Sri Harold Klemp. I had just moved to Portland a year earlier and the fallout here was by far the most intense because Darwin Gross had a house near here in Oak Grove and had a loyal band of followers.

For several months we were all in a state of limbo. People were groping around for hidden meanings, not really knowing what to make of this business between the two Masters. After all, we were in Eckankar – this wasn't supposed to be happening to us. But as the weeks and months passed our bubble of the perfect spiritual path burst wide open like a stinking, rotten egg. The after birth of this event can only be described as "insane."

I decided to stay on as an official member of the organization but, at the same time I supported Sri Darwin Gross openly and without guilt and shame. I even subscribed to this his monthly newsletter he started issuing. A year after the excommunication startling things began happening. Eckists were pressured, manipulated, and even threatened with loss of membership if they continued supporting Sri Darwin.

Again, as before, Eckankar was not walking its talk when it truly mattered. In the Portland, Oregon Satsang (community of followers) group two Higher Initiates took it upon themselves to put a blow-torch to Sri Darwin's pictures, tapes, books, and everything else having to do with him. I still feel utter outrage to this book burning event even after all these years.

Like the rational and reasonable person I am, I drafted a letter (with the other witnesses) to Sri Harold outlining what we saw and asked how this could be. Within three weeks myself and the other two people got an official letter from the Eckankar office in Menlo Park, California, telling us that all our initiations were removed, our membership in Eckankar was terminated, and that we couldn't represent ourselves as Eckists anymore privately or publically.

No reason was ever given. Just a very short paragraph signed by an office staff person. I took the letter to the Portland Area Higher Initiate-in-Charge but was met with the coldest, loudest silence I ever experienced in my life. She told me to "stay away from the Eck Center or we will have you removed." I wrote two followup letters asking for immediate clarification on the matter. I never received any reply.

Since I had already drawn the conclusion that Sri Darwin was getting the shaft by the corporation, I declared my full public allegiance to him in October 1984. I always felt comfortable supporting the underdog so taking sides with Sri Darwin didn't take much thought. I really did believe (at the time) he was the innocent victim in all of this drama.

The following five years ended up being a transition period for me. It also gave me time to mourn the loss of my life as an Eckist. During this time the Eckankar corporation painted Sri Darwin as this "evil, malignant tumor that needed to be surgically removed" – as stated by most of the 8th Initiates at the time.

Sri Darwin's band of followers painted the other side as "little Hitlers." We all closed ranks around Sri Darwin as spiritual shields to protect him.

But he eventually just sat back and didn't do much of anything except whine like a baby about the whole event. We needed and wanted him to rebuild an organization or community that we all wanted so desperately. He masterfully played the hapless victim to the hilt.

In a letter from my friend and fellow traveler, Barry Mallet, in a letter dated 9-29-91 he stated bluntly: "Got a brochure from Darwin's group today. In it there's a paragraph that says, 'Sri Darwin holds the Eck Rod of Power and lives in a mountain retreat on the Oregon coast and a little hut in the South Pacific.' So what the hell is he doing with the Rod of Power – sitting on it? Gimme a big F-ing break!!!

The above was indeed a common complaint from most of those who followed Darwin out of Eckankar. Barry Mallet went on to say in that same letter, the following:

"I sat here all morning trying to write a letter to Darwin that wouldn't sound like I was foaming at the mouth when I wrote it. Finally, I just gave up. I wanted to ask him to help me understand why he wasn't better organized and active. Why hasn't he provided more dynamic leadership for those who he encouraged to leave Eckankar and follow him? What is the point of his efforts in the courts to re-establish himself if he is going to be so ambivalent about the whole damn business?"

And further yet in Barry Mallet's long letter, he stated: "The thing that has always frustrated me about Darwin was his habit of never giving you a straight answer to anything. I can't stand Sri Harold's effeminate personality, his dishonesty, his sophistry, and misrepresentation. And for Darwin, I see only the guy who blew us all off because he was more interested in being a Jazz musician than the Living Eck Master, then changed his mind and set himself up in the 'Guru business again' – then where is the path for me to follow?" And in a followup letter from me I couldn't disagree with my friend.

It was at this time that Sri Darwin personally elevated me to the 6th Initiation in a private ceremony in Oak Grove on the recommendation of my good friends Jerry & Joy W. It felt good after all those years in Eckankar to finally get this personal attention from the Master. And since he lived in the area it was not unusual to bump into him at coffee shops in the Northwest neighborhood. I had the privilege of having lunch with him several times. But even after receiving this initiation, I didn't feel any different or more empowered. It was as if we were merely going through ritualistic motions that was diffused of meaning.

Sri Darwin started pushing prosperity theology in his monthly messages to us and saying to "give and give until it hurts, and then give some more." He even had the audacity of telling several local followers, including a friend of mine who was quite well off financially, to open up those babk savings accounts and pensions for the "cause."

His reasoning seemed to be that he needed the bucks after all. And how could he minister to our spiritual needs if he couldn't live in the style he was used to in Eckankar. What he seemed to be yearning for was the glory days of Eckankar when he was the Master of a global following of 55,000 plus initiates, nice salary (including a generous expense account), car, and a private jet. I felt a deep sadness for the man at this point. Some of his staunchest supporters started bailing like rats leaving a sinking ship.

Sri Darwin announced shortly after this that he wanted each of us to become his distributors of the Black Pearls Herbal remedy. He wanted us all "to become rich with me." The only problem was that th FDA put out a warning the previous year about general health risks and possible tampering by overseas producers.

Product batches were found to have low levels of Benzodiazapines in them. Sri Darwin continued to aggressively push this product on us even in the face of the possible risks to people's health. Again, he needed the income to minister to our spiritual needs. He was still the Living Eck Master after all, so how could we question that? If this wasn't enough, several female Higher Initiates started coming forward talking about their sexual escapades with the man. They were of course feeling very used and tossed aside.

Who would blame these women? I guess having sex with him when he was a "legitimate all-powerful Master of an International movement" was one thing, but now he was just an ordinary guy, down on his luck, roaming the streets of Portland, with a handful of loyal students.

The glamour bubble was gone and we all saw the kinks, wrinkles and blemishes of just a mere human being. I thank these seven women for having the courage to come forward with their stories of Darwin's sexual abuses. Once again it proved Sri Darwin's real intent: do as I say, not as I do, and don't question.

This was the straw that broke the camels back for me (and others). For years there had been persistent rumors about Sri Darwin's sexual appetite and his abuse of pain killers after many back surgeries.

I guess I chose to ignore this stuff initially, somehow thinking that if it was true then there must be a higher purpose to it.

Being aware of this man's flaws, and thinking it was tied to a higher purpose is the kind of irrational cult thinking a True Believer engages in. Thank goodness I finally saw the error of my ways in this regard. It was the summer of 1988 when this inner separation snapped like an over stretched rubber band. I quit bothering with the man and his religion and his constant whining. The next year I got around to writing him a letter in September 1989 and quite literally told him to "go to hell." I have never looked back with any remorse.

It was at this time I completely threw all the ingrained thinking about Eckankar history, theology and so-called ethics on the rubbish heap where it belonged.

I have not regretted this decision for a moment.

In March of 2008, Mr. Darwin Gross passed away due to diabetes, drug addiction and a host of other health concerns. He died a very broken man with only a couple of dozen loyal friends around him. When I heard this news, I did feel a deep sadness for him but that's all.

SOME AFTER THOUGHTS ABOUT ECKANKAR AND SOUL TRAVEL

Most people who report "astral travel," "soule travel." or "OBE" describe a vivid sense of leaving the body and perceiving the world from an external vantage point – sometimes floating above a bed, a chair, moving through walls, or visiting distant locals. While the True Believers claim these experiences as "proof," research in psychology and neuroscience offers plausible mechanisms that can generate the same compelling experience without requiring the mind to literally depart the brain.

A key point is that soul travel is not typically experienced as an act of one's imagination. It can feel perceptually rich, emotionally intense, and logically coherent – qualities that our brain usually associates with genuine perception. But the feeling of reality is itself a brain-generated judgment, built from sensory cues, memory, attention, and expectation. Under certain conditions – especially at the boundary between sleep and wakefulness – those same systems can produce a convincing model of being located outside the body.

1. One of the strongest scientific links to "soul travel" is the sleep cycle, particularly REM (rapid eye movement) sleep. Thus Eckankar's obsession with dreams.

2. One's sense of being located "inside" one's body is not a direct reading of a soul's coordinates; it is an ongoing construct sometimes called the *body schema* or body model. The brain continuously integrates signals from vision, touch, position of limbs, and balance and motion to decide where "I" am in space. When these inputs conflict or become unreliable -
 – as can happen in sleep transitions, extreme fatigue, illness, meditation, anesthesia, or high stress – the brain may update the self-model in highly unusual ways. A common result is a shift in perceived self-location (feeling detached, enlarged, shrunken, or displaced), which can be experienced as hovering, drifting, flying, or viewing the body from elsewhere. Clinical and experimental work supports this idea: disruptions in regions that integrate multisensory information about the body and perspective – soul travel.

3. Another psychological pathway to soul travel involves dissociation – experiences such as, "I feel unreal or detached from myself" and "the world feels unreal." Dissociation can occur during panic, prolonged stress, grief, trauma reminders, or sensory overload, and it is thought to reflect the brain's attempts to reduce overwhelming emotion by creating distance from immediate experience. Because the sense of self is partly anchored in bodily feelings, that "distance" can be interpreted spatially: the person may feel as if they are watching themselves from the outside, as if the self has stepped away from the body.

4. The brain does not only generate sensations; it interprets them using prior beliefs. If someone expects soul travel – through spiritual teachings, online forums, spiritual exercises, guided meditations, or other type of tutorials -

– ambiguous bodily sensations during drowsiness (tingling, heaviness, rushing sounds, hypnotic jerks, etc.) may be labeled as signs of separation. Expectation also shapes what is noticed and remembered. Because memory is reconstructive, later retelling can become more coherent and narrative-like, and people may selectively emphasize details that felt meaningful, while forgetting mismatches. None of this implies dishonesty; it only reflects how human perception and memory normally work.

Taking all four points together, this naturalistic account does not deny that soul travel can feel profound or life-changing; it suggests that the source of the experience is the mind's remarkable capacity to simulate a self in space – sometimes, under unusual conditions.

PART 3
SEX IS EVIL, SEX IS DEATH

After my disturbing experience with Eckankar one would think I had enough of spiritual masters. Right? Wrong! Unless you have been there it's very difficult for most people to understand what drives another so passionately in search of the Holy Grail. I have found in my own life this passionate drive was fueled by a hyper-fundamentalist worldview of what the truth should be, and not what reality actually is. It took Martin Marty's massive multi-volume *Fundamentalism Project* to drive this truth home. I found that whether it's Christianity, Eckankar, the New Age, Buddhism, Islam, or even Marxism, the fires of fundamentalism and pre-scientific thinking cook under most social, religious and political movements.

As I said previously in the last section, I gave up on the whole Eckankar worldview in 1989. I felt I still needed a spiritual community to call home, so I signed on with the Science of Spirituality in November of that same year. And since I had already experimented with vegetarianism in the past, the groups diet restriction didn't bother me.

This group was under the leadership of Sant Rajinder Singh, Kirpal Singh's grandson. Successorship had been handed down from father to son to grandson. How's that for a medieval-style nepotism? And yes, they had developed quite a complex argument to rationalize this. In a nutshell their explanation was that this was a "rare first time in human history that the God-power was passed through three generations of the same family." And this was not to be questioned further.

I didn't stay with this group very long. What really spooked me were statements like: "Sex is evil, sex is death." believe it or not this phrase by Kirpal Singh is peppered through out his books. Knowing this I still sought and received initiation in March 1990. But from that moment on life became hell for me. The only two times I went to their Burch Bay Retreat Facility in Washington state, was like attending an old fashion Christian camp meeting with lots of mutual pats on the back and how we were better than those "worldly people." Where did I hear that before?

One of the reasons for the fundamentalist atmosphere of this group was that it was heavily dominated by former ultra conservative Jews, who signed on with Kirpal Singh back back in the late nineteen sixties. They were now the group's leadership up and down the West coast of the United States. Even some of the practices of conservative Judaism filtered into the group's teachings, such as draping a white cloth over the head during meditation.

When I started having personal difficulties with the Portland leader, Lenny S., others just told me to get along and defer to him on everything because "he's an older and wiser Satsangi brother." The man treated me like garbage, as if I was his personal servant.

He was raised a conservative Jew and grew up in Brooklyn, New York. He had lots of very old fashion ideas and attitudes about women and "underlings" like me. One day he even wanted me to come to his house and do yard work without any compensation saying, "it's good for your spiritual growth and builds character." He still insisted I do this even though I was between jobs and needed the money.

The way he acted and talked down to people in general was horrible. The caretakers of the Burch Bay Retreat Center agreed with me very ardently on this man's negative and disruptive attitude, but simply mouthed the party line of "deferring to your elders who are older and wiser in all matters." Their rationalization of the emotional abuse I suffered from this man was that it built spiritual stamina and character. I won't go into all the examples of how this man humiliated and abused me privately as well as in public, and how the organization gave him shade. I left this group in November 1990.

PART 4
FROM INDIA WITH LOVE

What made me increasingly unhappy with the Science of Spirituality was that it was not *science* at all. Just faith-based opinions and visions covered in the mantle of "science." Eckankar did the same thing, calling their teachings the "Science of Soul travel." No science their at all.

Anyway, in my continued search for the Holy Grail, I came across other Satsangs that were different versions of the Light and Sound teachings. I came across a Satsang in Soamibagh, India, that was represented by Shiv Dayal Singh, the August Founder of these different offshoots or branches, back in the 19th century. I realized I may be on the right track to find the mother of all Light and Sound teachings – the original, the real McCoy.

The many branches all claimed to be the one true line of succession.

I had read Dr. Julian Johnson's books in 1978, which were written from the perspective of the Beas lineage of the Radhasoami teachings. The Science of Spirituality was a member of this Beas lineage, but there was something mighty narrow and rigid about the succession of gurus all being Sikhs. More nepotism but broader based , I thought to myself? I was looking for the real stuff so to speak. I wanted to get as close to the original truth of the Radhasoami teachings as I could possibly get. It just so happened my wish came true.

I happened upon the original teachings of Shiv Dayal Singh quite by accident in October 1989 while browsing the book section of the Portland Goodwill store. I came across a 1958 English edition of *Sar Bachan Prose* published in Soami Bagh, India by the PARENT-LINE SATSANG (RAHDASOAMI FAITH).

When I opened this book and saw the photos of Soami Bagh's five primary gurus, my eyes popped wide open. I had never seen these gurus before and they were NOT Sikhs.

I had always thought that the Beas Satsang was the mother of all Radhasoami sects but I was wrong. It was a month later that I found the entire set of *Correspondence With Certain Americans* by Sant Das, at Powell's City of Books. I devoured these books like a thirsty man out in the desert finding a jug of ice water. It seemed that the Agra group was indeed the mother of all Radhasoami groups, the Holy Grail if you will. The only downside was that they had been without a "manifest Master" since 1948. Their explanation from their last guru was that an indefinite period of "interregnum" would follow.

In April 1990, I dashed off a letter to Agra for more updated information. It took a couple of months to receive a reply. A Mr. Nirmal Das Maheshwari sent me a nice response and updated book list. He was the eldest son of Sant Das, an important figure at Soami Bagh, who died in 1983. What started was a long correspondence that virtually educated me on many sects and the traditions and ideas of Radhasoami Faith. My biggest concern was the absence of a living guru. But it was explained to me that since Babuji Maharaji's death in 1948, the current guru decided to stay "unmanifested until proper time."

But after reading the many Agra books it seemed rather obvious that those in the West as well as a faction inside India considered Sant Das as the last guru. Even his son, Nirmal Das, did not deny this!

On December 29, 1991, I received a letter from Paul G., a Radhasoami Satsangi from Klamath Falls, Oregon. He had visited Sant Das in 1978 and got initiated. Like myself, Paul was a former Eckist. He had just got back from a four month visit to Soami Bagh. In his letter he stated: "It has been 40-plus years since the last manifest Sat Guru (Babuji Maharaj). You can perhaps imagine the impact on morale among most Satsangis not to mention the divisions of opinions and motivations. Most elder Satsangis of Babuji's time have since passed on and for many Satsangis today it is a hereditary association. There are a number of so-called factions owing allegiances to one person or another, if any. All of this is, of course, by grace and for the very best of reasons. In time, soon I hope, the true Guru will manifest and those Satsangis with a genuine inclination for truth will realize their good fortunes."

Another paragraph from Paul's letter states: "I have never met another Satsangi here in America, although I have met several Indians living in America when I attended Bhandaras (religious festivals) in India. There are a few Westerners such as Mr. William Collias. When in Soami Bagh I met two elder Satsangi ladies from Brazil and I know of 3 in France. In 1978 I talked to a few Satsangis in California and Sant Das had written to me once that a Satsangi had moved up to Grants Pass, Oregon. The Indians are mostly on the East coast (New Jersey) and I know of a few in Missouri and Texas. In the late 60's there were a number of Satsangis, and they would gather for Bhandaras but didn't seem to hold a close relationship to one another. Perhaps that's important due to the interregnum (the time period between Manifest Gurus).

Finding out this information made me feel quite alone, without a community of fellow believers here, didn't make me feel so good because I was looking for an instant community that I could engage with.

I received an werogramme from Nirmal das dated 4-22-92, saying he was coming to the USA for a visit and I should contact Paul G. about setting up a time at my house for snacks and tea. I was ecstatic! Electrified would be the better word, however. I had already made the decision to ask for initiation and decided that Nirmal Das was indeed the unmanifested Sat Sant Guru. I had the same feeling about him as I did when I first found Eckankar. It seemed I went full circle and was finally coming home.

One month later I received a phone call from Paul concerning Nirmal Das' visit. We talked in length about the details, time and date. We agreed the visit would be at 11:00 am on a Tuesday next month.

It would be an all afternoon affair.
Paul suggested I have plenty of
black tea and milk on hand for
Nirmal and his wife, as this has been
largely their diet while traveling.
Paul really impressed upon me that
Nirmal Das and his wife were
traveling as tourists and did not
want to be pestered by personal
questions on his "status at Soami
Bagh." But then again Paul made it
abundantly clear that he believed
Nirmal Das to be the unmanifested
Sat Sant Guru. Paul also told me
that I must have some "really great
karma" because Nirmal Das NEVER
goes to the homes of non-Satsangis.
The reader can imagine how this
made me feel.

The great day finally arrived!
Tuesday, June 2, 1992. It was a
clear, sunny day, about 73 degrees
with a slight breeze. I had green
and black tea ready to be boiled.

Cinnamon coated graham crackers would be the snacks. Paul called at 11:45 saying they were just leaving Newport and would get to my place as soon as they could. Everyone finally arrived at 4:30 pm. I was disappointed that we could only visit for two hours but that was enough. Even five minutes with the man would have suited me.

Nirmal Das was wearing a gray-green leisure suit with sandals. Everyone took off foot wear at the door. He looked a lot like his father Sant Das. It took me nearly ten minutes to adjust to his clipped and fast, Indian-style English. Mrs. Maheshwari did not speak English at all and was mostly silent during the whole visit. I did notice her looking around at the decor and seemed rather curious about our two cats. I wished I could have talked with her directly. The few words she did say were the typical hello and thank you. She was dressed in a very beautiful sari with braided hair, and looked a lot younger than her husband, who I believe was in his early sixties. She smiled a lot and listened eagerly when her husband spoke.

Paul, who I met for the first time, was dressed for the summer weather, as though he just stepped off the golfing greens. He had long pants, a conservative sport shirt, closely cropped hair, mustache, and by and large, very professional looking. I was in complete contrast to him: long beard, tie-dyed shirt and mountain shorts. I felt a little out of place, but oh well. As they all made themselves at home I started the tea. Nirmal Das then patted the couch next to him and said: 'sit."

He brought out typed instruction sheets on how to conduct personal Satsang privately and went over these points several times. He then gave me large photographs of the gurus in bright color. Also, he gave me a small snapshot of Babuji Maharaj reclining in bed with the phrase below: Radhasoami Dayal Ki Daya Radhasoami Sahai. After putting it in my hand he squeezed real firmly and stared intently into my eyes. The energy that shot up my spine was awesome. I seemed to be at once adrift outside my body, looking down on all four of us.

To this day I still haven't quite figured out how this happened and what physiological triggers were pressed. It is just one of those unexplained events. Nirmal Das then brought out two baggies of "Prashad" – candies blessed by the Guru. (In the absence of a manifest Guru the candies are put upon a surviving article of clothing of the last manifested guru and thereby blessed. At Soami Bagh in Agra these candies are made and fifty pound sacks are piled upon the burial sarcophagus for at least thirty minutes.) we all shared some and then he told me to put the rest away for my own use later. I was to nibble on some daily as I chanted the word "Radhasoami" inwardly as *Radh-a-so-am-i,* in five distinct syllables.

One candy was called "saltish" and the other "laddus." It was different but good. He then offered me a small glass vile of Charnamrit" – water blessed in the same fashion as the candies in Agra. He instructed me in its use and told me to add several drops per gallon of tap water to be used daily. (Thank god it wasn't spittle like the gurus of old used.) Paul just sat there with his mouth wide open because Nirmal Das was treating me like a seasoned Satsangi brother.

We then went to the dining room for tea, which had to be reheated again. Nirmal Das and his wife ate with gusto and really liked the cinnamon grahams. In her nervousness Mrs. Maheshwari spilled tea everywhere but it was okay. I couldn't believe the amount of sugar they dumped into their tea cups. I had some herbal teas and sugarless snacks but these remained untouched. Nirmal das actually put three black tea bags in his mug and then added eight teaspoons of sugar and then milk. Wow! I get a headache now remembering that.

He discussed in great detail of all the "mischief" at Soami Bagh regarding the position and status of his father, Sant Das. He went on about how certain council members were accusing him of making his father into a guru. He went into more detail about all the cliques and factions and the councils refusal to budge on anything.

Everyone finally left at 6:45 pm. We all exchanged bows and folded hands several times as I saw them to their car. As their car pulled away down the street I stood their for almost five minutes, wishing they would come back. My head was in the clouds for weeks afterward. For thirteen days following this visit I had a rough time sleeping at night due to strange dreams and physical sensations.

The energies would start flowing every time I closed my eyes. That very odd sensation of ants crawling up my spine persisted for several months, especially when I meditated. It was almost distracting at times, especially at work. The Nirmal Das visit produced in me inner peace. I just knew I had encountered a great soul. I also knew that I wanted to get initiated right away.

Within three weeks of the visit I sent a petition to the Secretary of Soami Bagh requesting initiation as outlined in the papers Nirmal left.

I sent a carbon copy to Nirmal Das. He then "facilitated the process" with Satsang Authorities.

On July 13, 1992, Secretary, Dr. B.P. Saxena recognized my petition and asked me to fill out a formal application for initiation and dispatch it immediately. On July 17th I got a letter from Nirmal Das stating he had consulted with Dr. Saxena and the "process would definitely facilitated in timely manner."

On August 14, 1992, I received the following letter from Dr. B.P. Saxena: Thanks for your letter through Sri N.D. Masheshwari. I am glad to know that you are cherishing a desire to be initiated in Radhasoami Faith and you have full faith in Dhwanatmak Name of Supreme Being. I have sanctioned you the initiation of both updesh. The first of Sumiran and Dhyan and the second of Bhajan

(Surat Shabd Yoga Abhyas). You must work hard with the first updesh and until and unless, you get proficiency in the first, you would not have much gain in the second. After few months of practice, of first updesh, you may devote some time for the second updesh after practicing the first on every day and then you may inform me with the experiences, if you have any. I am sending herewith the papers of both the updeshes, which please go through them. You may keep them for some time but you will please return it to me after you have satisfied yourself. More on hearing from you. With Hearty Radhasoami, Affectionately, Dr. B.P. Saxena."

Up to this point I had been meditating two hours daily, chanting the word Radhasoami inwardly, silently. Once I was "sanctioned" my inner experiences seemed to magnify beyond all belief.

I had some rather strange but positive experiences. At least a dozen times the image of Sant Das would appear during meditation and sit next to me and talk about Radhasoami principles. Twice he touched my forehead which produced this brilliant white flashing light. His touched seemed real.

Boy, when I hallucinate I don't mess around. Of course, looking back on these experiences with cold, calculating observation, I know that they were caused by my intense meditation, readings, chanting, and pondering, and a whole lot of wish fulfillment. They were the end result of psycho-physiological changes to my nervous system, nothing more.

In December 1992 I received my first official "tin of Prashad" – candies blessed by the Guru. In it was more saltish, and laddus, as well as Charnamrit. It was a good Christmas.

I also received more free books from Nirmal Das. Up until now he had sent me four free books over the past year as "gifts." And now more. The book, *Interregnum*, which had been compiled from all of Sant Das' books went a long way in explaining the big gulf of time without a manifest guru. In the Soami Bagh tradition of guru succession the previous one doesn't tidily leave documents stating who the successor will be. The next guru emerges by "force of presence" until the general Satsang openly recognizes him or her.

From the beginning of my correspondence with Nirmal Das, I had always felt a kinship with him. And why he bestowed all those gifts on me I'll never know. There must have been worthier subjects than me. The mere fact that he visited my home when I was a non-satsangi speaks volumes about who he was.

For the next year I faithfully practiced my meditation and read all the books many times over. But it wasn't enough. I was lonely. When you're on a spiritual path you need community (for awhile, anyway) for that emotional support. At this point a spiritual community of R.S. satsangis was completely non-existent, except for Paul G. and he lived in Klamath Falls.

There was an elderly satsangi called Mr. William Collias, who had been a Satsangi for over thirty years with a dozen visits to Soami Bagh under his belt. But he was physically frail and in poor health and was never receptive to a visit nor correspondence after that first letter. Attempting to practice a spiritual path in a vacuum is difficult if not downright impossible (in my case, that is). Even the scores of letters from Nirmal Das didn't alleviate the loneliness.

Many problems arose with my study of the Parent-Line of Radhasoami Faith.

Firstly, the entire faith seemed to be based on this hyper-fundamental worldview. "We are right, they are wrong!" The other R.S. sects were not recognized nor their satsangis considered fellow brothers and sisters. "They are to be avoided at all cost." The modern world was to be avoided within reason.

Secondly, the faith seemed steeped in this legalistic jargon and hair-splitting of words on differences between other sects. For their purity of faith they received isolation and backwardness.

Thirdly, they still persisted in certain outrageous superstitious claims: the belief that Babuji Maharaj spent 19 months in his mother's womb, and Nirmal Das spent 14 months in his mothers womb.

They claim it was an "omen" sent from God in both cases. As I stated to Nirmal Das in a letter: "if this medical miracle was true then both accounts would have made headlines around the globe." He said I would have to accept the truth of both accounts on faith and "never question it further."

I decided to lay low and start looking for a spiritual community to fellowship with. I stopped my correspondence temporarily with Nirmal Das.

PART 5
BUDDHA AIN'T HERE ANYMORE

I took a sabbatical from the Radhasoami faith to pursue my interests in Soto Zen Buddhism because locally they offered a spiritual community which I was desperate for, and I liked the fact they put any concept of an after life on hold for the "here and now."

One Sunday morning I visited the Dharma Rain Zen Center in Southeast Portland to alleviate this loneliness. The people were nice and welcoming. I had already studied Buddhism in an academic sense but had never *practiced* it. Most of what I knew about Buddhism was from the writings of Alan Watts and Paul Reps. Both these gentlemen presented Buddhism in an informal way and practice.

Dharma Rain taught the Soto Zen School of Buddhism and their lineage came from the Buddhist group at Mt. Shasta Abbey in northern California.

Soto Zen trends to be monastic and formalist in nature, and the folks at Dharma Rain scoffed at Alan Watts even being a real Buddhist. That was my first red flag, but I needed a community and this seemed rather minor in the great scheme of things.

For the next two years I poured my heart and soul into this teaching, attended Sunday service and a Wednesday study group, which in some ways seemed very Catholic-in-style to me. There was chanting, the incense, the prayers, the homily by the Abbot, and the social gathering afterwards. I looked forward to this Sunday Buddhist "mass".

I started taking classes on Wednesdays and went to all of the minor and major festival events, retreats and Buddhist holy day ceremonies. I became a regular in short order time and made a few friends. I also went through the ceremony of acceptance, becoming an official *Acolyte*, and my name was transcribed onto their lineage cloth. They even gave me a cool necklace with a knot at the end, made from black twisted cloth. This was to be worn during meditation, whether at center or at home.

Eventually it had to happen: *the money!*

I was unemployed at the time but was able to donate a few bucks here and there, especially during the high Buddhist holidays. One of the senior members who was also on the board of directors pulled me aside and asked that I commit to a specific monthly donation to the center. After all, I was an official member now and needed to support "our family."

He asked that I donate $30 monthly. I was floored and told him I was temporarily unemployed but could still give $10 monthly.

He seemed satisfied and never spoke to me again about it. I was left with the odd feeling that I was letting everyone down at the center, and that I should personally sacrifice to help out. After several two months, certain senior members attempted to broach the subject with me and I always gave the same answer. I was jobless and struggling. I even volunteered my time doing chores around the center to waylay my guilt they imposed upon me.

After nine months of this I approach the head Abbot for a personal meeting (which was a $25 fee for a fifteen-minute session). He was quite accommodating in his attitude and seemed genuinely concerned about my plight. The outcome was that as soon as I get work I needed to "make regular donations to the center." After this meeting the pressure was on big time, and so was my guilt.

Every time I talked with someone it always ended up about money. I fully understand that it takes money to keep the center going and to pay a small stipend to the Abbot. But as soon as I became an official member the whole path changed for me. I wasn't looked upon anymore as a mere outsider who came to visit and meditate. Part of the problem I saw in the over-handed way of asking for money, was the fact that nearly all the senior members were way above my economic and social class: doctors, lawyers, teachers, engineers, therapists. Social workers, and self-employed business people.

It seemed not a week went by without a red flag going up with me. My relationship with the center started seriously degrading over the last six months. Sometimes I wouldn't even attend a service for several weeks. I finally got the opportunity to walk to the bus stop with a regular visitor at the center. I'll call him "Mike."

Mike was a sixty-something man with long white hair and beard. Looked a lot like Santa Claus. He always looked so wise, serene and formidable sitting on his zen cushion during Sunday services. He always had this air of quiet authority about him. He had been attending every Sunday service for the past seven years but never committed to becoming an official member.

When I asked him why he gave me a thousand-yard stare and said, "Buddha ain't here anymore." "Then why do you keep coming", I asked. He just winked at me and said the place helps him stay off drugs. So Mike was using the practice as his own unique replacement for Narcotics Anonymous. At the time I remember telling him, "Whatever floats your boat."

He further added that it's best to stay on the periphery of religion and do the practice, because once you commit to the organization then that's all it becomes – an organizational affair. Mike gave me a nugget of wisdom that I have not forgotten to this day. My initial estimate of the man was correct: he was very wise indeed! After this encounter I never went back to Dharma Rain Center. I quietly disappeared from sight and went on with my life.

PART 6
BECOMING HUMAN AGAIN

By the summer of 1994 I was once again at a crossroads in my life. I had given up completely writing regularly to Nirmal Das for almost two years. He stopped sending the tins of Prashad. I neglected answering a few important letters and then stopped responding altogether. It was at this time I also stopped going to the Zen Center. I was in a really big spiritual funk.

It was at this time a book by Paul Kurtz (Professor of Philosophy at SUNY), The *Transcendental Temptation*, had a moving and profound impact on my thinking. The freedom and liberation I have always sought seemed to jump off the pages of this book. He spoke of the myths and the legends and the uselessness of striving for a Holy Grail that wasn't there. He also spoke of the happiness gained from taking responsibility for our own life and not turning it over to some guru or organization.

I certainly achieved a sense of freedom upon finishing the massive tome.

So this ended my life as a New Age devotee. Regrettably, I didn't formerly withdraw from the R.S. Faith right away but just went on with my life. It wasn't until June 1997 that I sent a formal letter of resignation to Nirmal Das and Dr. B.P. Saxena. I actually had tears in my eyes upon finishing the letter and dropping it in the mailbox. I stood at that mailbox for over fifteen minutes before sliding the letter in, and then wiping the tears with my sleeve.

You see, by writing that letter I gave up twenty-five years of seeking, a lifetime of involvement in seeking a Holy Grail. This kind of attachment is the hardest thing to let go, I think the Buddha knew this; that's why most of his teachings dwell on the giving up on desire.

I became convinced that the whole guru-disciple relationship, and those spiritual groups that still pushed this concept, was simply an anachronism in today's modern world. Following this inner revelation I went through a two year period (1997-1999) of cleaning out my psyche of all the garbage of my past. It was like emptying a glass of water and then slowly putting back in a little bit at a time. When it was all over I felt relieved, clean and with the feeling of elation.

After this mental cleaning exercise I went on a reading binge of humanist-oriented literature. In particular I studied the writings of John Dewey, Sidney Hook, Corliss Lamont, Martin Gardner, Milton Rothman, Susan Blackmore, and Paul Kurtz. All I can say is – "what an education." The beginning of the end of my personal *transcendental temptation* was an established fact.

In the autumn of 1996, I had enough of the New Age hocus-pocus and resolved not to get involved in it again. While sipping an espresso at a local coffee shop in downtown Portland, I came to the terrifying revelation that I had wasted the first half of my life in a senseless pursuit of something not there.

The Holy Grail was a myth and for the first time in my life it didn't have power over me and I felt the overwhelming sense of my own eventual extinction. For three weeks following this epiphany, I walked about like someone in a fog. I felt a bit disoriented. Then a second big revelation hit me even harder than the first. I had a lot to live for. I could make a difference right here and now and help create a higher level of ethical civilization.

I reflected upon my many years of work with the homeless population and my environmental projects.

This took on a whole new meaning for me. I could now devote myself to these causes without some authority figure telling me what to do and how to do it. I did not have to fear a big guy in heaven with a big stick that might get made at me for doing it my way. For most of my life I felt I had an albatross around my neck like the ancient mariner in that classic poem. Now I had a perfect sense of what philosopher Paul Kurtz called "exuberance."

It was at this point I sat down and wrote out on paper a vision statement for myself. Something tangible on paper that would help me move forward. It was a therapeutic exercise suggested to me by a Soto Zen Buddhist Priest, and since then has become my personal compass in life.

My personal philosophy of life is a system of convictions and practices offering a pragmatic skepticism as a method of inquiry, evolutionary Darwinism as a cosmic worldview, naturalistic morality as a life ethic, and democratic pluralism as a social polity. It is an integrative approach to living life to the fullest, leading to happiness, peace of mind, and a feeling of oneness with nature.

The vision statement I wrote down was unique in that I didn't merely accept someone's worldview all packaged up nicely with a big bow, with rules and regulations on how to live. I made sure that my new vision of life was future-oriented and reflected my own concerns, hopes and dreams in an ever-changing modern world.

Reflecting on my long journey from die-hard theist to humanist to radical agnostic and my unsuccessful search for a theory of everything, I am glad that it took me years to accomplish. If it had happened overnight I might have become so emotionally unhinged and intellectually paralyzed, that I might have succumbed to suicide, drugs or alcohol to cope with such profound change.

I no longer run after the hot new guru, political cause or religious ideology of the day to give me answers. From the moment my search began in the pastor's office library until the day I declared myself *FREE*, I have come to realize that whatever outward ideology I followed, however different they were, I was still a fundamentalist in my worldview.

In the words of Martin Marty, who founded the "Fundamentalism Project" at the University of Chicago, School of Religion, "Every new Utopian political ideology, spirituality, and even the various UFO/Abductee cults, founded inn the 20th century, has been deeply connected to the fundamental worldview. It is this fundamentalism that fears modernity, technology and the shifting of planetary values that herald an uncertain future."

I leave the reader with this exhortation:

*In my experience of spiritual seeking, I've found that spiritual communities tend to factionalize and become corrupt, and finally just organizations – that serve only the organization. The individual becomes a human cash register for organizational power. The true seeker eventually needs to **walk alone** in their search for inner meaning.*

PART 7
THE ROAD AHEAD

My Life Stance now is to live with clear-eyed wonder and steady purpose: to understand what moves me, to accept what I cannot control, and to offer what I can. From Spinoza, I take the discipline of seeking adequate understanding – seeing myself as part of nature rather than set apart from it. When I trace causes instead of clinging to blame or resentment, my emotions loosen their grip and I return to a calmer power of acting. I try to follow my conatus – the inner striving to persist and flourish – not as self-centered ambition, but as a commitment to grow in reason, generosity, and joy. In this view, freedom is not getting everything I want; it is wanting wisely, in harmony with reality. The Japanese philosophy of *mono no aware* gives that harmony a softer texture: the recognition that everything I love is transient, and therefore luminous. I try to meet beauty with gratitude rather than possession, to let endings teach tenderness instead of despair. The other Japanese philosophy of Ikigai grounds these actions in the everyday. My purpose is not a single grand title; it is the small, repeatable alignment of what I care about, what I can do well, what others genuinely need, and what sustains my life. So I aim to build habits that keep me useful and awake: deep work, honest relationships, care for my body, and attention to the present moment. When I live this way, my days feel both humble and sacred – an ongoing practice of understanding, appreciating, and contributing.

ABOUT THE AUTHOR

The author refers to himself as a 71-year old grumpy white guy who is in recovery from prostate cancer and has Type-2 diabetes. He also has an attitude the size of the Grand Canyon and a sense of wonder as big as the Milky Way galaxy. During his younger years he was never one to settle down to a safe existence on the assembly line and chasing after the almighty corporate dollar. He mostly lived on the outer fringes of polite society.

Then all of a sudden, he woke up one morning in his 40th year and realized he was old.

Some things about his youth have not changed and hopefully never will. Not being the type of person to chase the dollar for a safe existence, he spent most of his working life as a social services worker and sometimes political activist.

Currently he is semi-retired after 25-plus years in the grocery business. He still works part-time to "stay in the game" for as long as he can.

For the past 28-years he has been *unaffiliated* from all political parties and religious organizations, and has come to the conclusion that all political parties and religions are simply corporate whores, who have more interest in a narrow moneyed agenda than the people they claim to serve. However, philosophically speaking, he considers himself a New England Liberal when it comes to politics.

He has volunteered for many causes in the past, including the right to privacy, decriminalization of marijuana, death with dignity, and a woman's right to make her own decisions on her health care.

His cultural interests include

Celtic folk music, the old English comedies on BBC America, foreign films (especially by the renowned and late director, Akira Kurosawa), and the theater. He is widely read in many journals in literature, politics, science, and religion.

For the past 40-years he has been living in the Concordia neighborhood of northeast Portland, Oregon. He has a life partner, Ave Marie, and one dog and four cats which keeps him busy. The time he has left is used to create tall tales to amuse himself and others.

CONTACT INFO

Email:
mercuryflatsgazette@gmail.com

Book Page:
https://bendouglassbooks.com

on the margins of what Kenneth Rexroth called "the social lie." It's with the dropouts, misfits, dissidents, renegades, and revolutionaries, against the grain, between the cracks and among the enemies of the state that the good stuff can be found.

Fortunately, there is a mighty subterranean river of testimony from the disaffected, a large cache of hidden history, of public secrets overlooked by the drab conventional wisdom the *Mercury Flats Publishing* aims to tap into. A little something to set against the crushed hopes, mountains of corpses, and commodification of everything. We think, it's the best thing Western Civilization has going for itself.

VERDANA FONT -
Usage/Design/History

Verdana is a humanist sans-serif typeface designed by Matthew Carter in 1996 for Microsoft, optimized for exceptional legibility on screen at small sizes. It features a large x-height, wide proportions, and loose spacing, making it ideal for web design and email, though it was designed for screens, it has been used in branding, famously by IKEA.

This font was used for the book you are reading so that in the future it can easily be transferred to a digital format.

READER NOTES

READER NOTES